In The Quiet Hours

A collection of poems

Antara sen

BookLeaf
Publishing

India | USA | UK

Copyright © Antara sen
All Rights Reserved.

This book has been self-published with all reasonable efforts taken to make the material error-free by the author. No part of this book shall be used, reproduced in any manner whatsoever without written permission from the author, except in the case of brief quotations embodied in critical articles and reviews.

The Author of this book is solely responsible and liable for its content including but not limited to the views, representations, descriptions, statements, information, opinions, and references ["Content"]. The Content of this book shall not constitute or be construed or deemed to reflect the opinion or expression of the Publisher or Editor. Neither the Publisher nor Editor endorse or approve the Content of this book or guarantee the reliability, accuracy, or completeness of the Content published herein and do not make any representations or warranties of any kind, express or implied, including but not limited to the implied warranties of merchantability, fitness for a particular purpose.

The Publisher and Editor shall not be liable whatsoever...

Made with ❤ on the BookLeaf Publishing Platform
www.bookleafpub.in
www.bookleafpub.com

Dedication

For my parents, whose kindness and unflinching support
are the foundation of my journey.

Preface

In a world that often feels hurried and intimidating, these poems offer a gentle pause. Rooted in love, nature and human relationships, each poem is an invitation to slow down and appreciate the beauty that surrounds us.

Whether read in a quiet moment or shared with a loved one, may these words bring a smile to your heart and a bit of light to your day.

Acknowledgements

I would like to express my deepest gratitude to the readers who have take the time to buy and read my poems. Your support and engagement make all the effort worthwhile. I would also like to thank my father whose literary genius has been a guiding light in my life.

The Fallibility of Heroes

The tired man sits alone
In one of twenty cubicles
His back is hunched, his desk groans
Beneath files and books and articles

Caged within the walls of fate
The window is his only reprieve
Here he writes a love sonnet
A moment of peace, a chance to breathe

Today the afternoon lingers longer
The call upstairs, the snarling face
The shaking fist, the pointed fingers
Another job lost, a fall from grace

As twilight unfurls its lonely hues
His shoulders drooped, the man walks home
His only daughter, his favourite muse
Knows not of the approaching storm

Into the shadows he retreats
Please don't leave me, his daughter implores
She bares witness to his defeat
And the gentle click of a closing door

Her father, her hero, brought to his knees
By a world she could not comprehend
Her innocence lost at thirteen
Her lifetime spent in making amends

The Fisherman

Long ago in a beach town
She watched the blue water
Turn to shades of orange
Like a fire spreading through the waves
In rhythm with the sunset
Shall I take a picture for you?
She asked the rowing fisherman
He smiled and pointed to his heart
"I take my pictures here"

I wish you knew

I wish you knew
that even though our love
was an impossibility
I found solace in the certainty
that your heart was mine

Climbing trees and scraping knees

A sepia colored granular memory
A reckless dare to climb a tree

Foolhardy minds, untouched by fear
The brother climbs, his sister cheers

Under the falling leaves she waits
Flanked by Gulmohar and lemon shades

CRACK!, the sound of a falling branch
A great fall, bruised legs and arms

Scampering squirrels and children alike
Into the golden dusk take flight

These were the last of the innocents
Bruises, dettol and peppermints

Johari bazaar

Past the array of shops in Johari Bazaar
The street puts her sunburnt toes away
Folds a bandhani over her knees
And rests beside the remnants of the morning
Afternoon is a time of respite from the noise
The only movement is that from slanting sunlight and
fallen mogras
An unintentional voyeur, she watches the ancient
balconies above her
And remembers their stories

Jacaranda

Last evening I found
An unkempt garden
And a blooming Jacarandra tree

Under the stone paved walkway
clumps of green grass
defied the odds to seek the light

How beautiful it is
when nature strains through neglect
In such a grand way

A childhood lived in the hills

Days of fog and gum boots
Of wildflowers appearing overnight
Lighting up every avenue
Like a new beginning

Days of pressing cold fingers
Over steaming cups of hot tea
Salvias in sunset colors
Afternoons with Agatha Christie

Evening walks through the hills
Under daunting shades of deodars
Sizzling swirls of fried noodles
An apple pie in Landour

As evening dusk bleeds into night
Tales of the headless horseman
Hushed voices, hurried feet take flight
Towards the warm glow of the Tavern

A roaring fire hisses and pops
Whiskey and a crossword puzzle

Hot water bottles and woolen socks
This was a childhood lived in the hills

The house forsaken

Rusted spokes on padlocked gates
An insidious fog drifts on the canal
Haunting ripples call his name
Echoing through the forgotten walls

Behind latticed curtains a shadow stirs
Crescent moon hides behind clouds
Sounds of dancing feet are heard
From every nook of the neglected house

The villagers lock their doors in fright
A tale remembered, passed down through time
Of the house that once stood in the light
Pulsating with life and family ties

A secret concealed with the walls
A forbidden love, a silent plea
The daughter of the house still calls
For an unfulfilled destiny

Under the cloak of a sky of ink
To freedom, they planned their way
A chase, an evil reckoning
A vanishing without a trace

The truth is buried under the stars
Sinking deeper into the folds of time
Through our stories, their love endures
In the house that once stood in the light

For no one

The valley sparkles like scattered fireflies
Slowly changing to smoky shades of dawn
She performs for no one
Since the day you left
In the afternoon a fizz of lonely blue bottles
Hum and dance across the window panes
The sun casts shadows into empty rooms
Collecting memories of still days and stiller evenings,
Since the day you left
The trees have been gathering darkness
All the nights since you left

Dotties blessing

The path wound up a steep incline
Infested with purple petunias
A small house rose from the horizon
With windows reflecting the season's flowers

Here lived an eccentric named Aunty Dotty
Camouflaged in interiors of flowery chintz
On cool summer evenings when time shifted slowly
She'd invite her neighbors for her home brewed drink

A special concoction she called Dottie's blessing
Made with rum and vanilla, cinnamon and cloves
Poured in wine bottles for fermentation
Lined with homemade jams by the window

'Tourists!', she would say, wrapped in a cardigan
Eyes bloodshot, cigarette holder in hand
Shivering at the reminder of their grim presence
Permeating like mist through their sacred land

A Shepherds pudding sputtering on the stove
They talked of their favorite picnic spots
The Abbey, Fernhill, the Hunters cove
Places stolen, sold, turned into parking lots

The sloping tin roof rattled in the wind
Her neighbors walked home in the twilight
Fragile silhouettes moving through the mountains
Through her battered contours and helpless plight

A speck of dust

Walking in miles of freshly blown sand
In unearthly predawn light
Sunburn, windburn
Hair breathing the forest and salty air
Rain clouds looming in the horizon
Wind whipping up sand and twigs
Lightening bolt through leaden sky
Marooned in the midst of it all, a realization
We are but a speck of dust, a fleeting trace
In this infinite expanse of time and space

The slow life

Late at night when all was quiet
She sat on the wind battered deck of her villa
Scattered sounds of music drifted towards her
Making its way over the rustle of palm fronds
And the gentle slap and recession of the surf

Her days while shapeless were not without joy
She had her breakfast by the sea
As she watched weathered fisherman haul their nets
With calloused hands that have born
The weight of great distances and storms

In the evenings, she would meet the villagers
And listen to their stories of distant shores
They seemed content in their isolation from the world
And in their steadfast faith
that each day would be the same.

Maximum city

Buildings bounding over the horizon
In search of light

A death march of squalid slums
Spread-eagled in the West

Hawkers in American T shirts
Sell combs made in China

Peeling posters on crumbling walls
Talk of old protest stories

Heaving buses, regurgitating taxis
Heckle pedestrians

Illegal subletting of small corners
Spaces distributed in packets

Beggars and dogs litter every sidewalk
Battered from fights and disease

Middle class savings squandered
For a square foot of stale air

Fractured settlements upon an island
homesick for places left behind

City of Joy

A walk to Flurys on Sunday afternoon
Through poetry and puchkas on park street
Past the rattle of windmills outside Moulin Rouge
Mrs. Gomes orders a rum cake and chicken patty

In Trincas, members of the press
Discuss uprisings by minorities
Over beer and steaks and Charms cigarettes
They blame unionization for their poverty

An East wind gathers over Chowringhee
Bare footed footballers disperse to go home
Tibetan women with braids and prayer beads
Set up stalls to sell pork momos

Outside the university, a group of students
Debate the philosophies of Kanu Sanyal
Of when the bhadralok were cornered in crumbling
mansions
And blood red flags hung from every wall

In the Saturday club there still exists
The last vestiges of colonialism
Where turbaned waiters serve finger chips

And lament the rise of fascism

20

All in a day's work

Sluggish meetings under bright blue lights
Whirlwind of deadlines and expectations
Stagnant routines, suspended time
Platitudes and chasing perceptions

Emails on matters of life or death
Appraisals measure the price of your soul
Sick leaves served with a complimentary wreath
Monotony of days to the same drumroll

Sunrise

This morning
The sun didn't rise
It was stitched back together
With golden clouds
breathing the sky back to life

The Matriarch

In a white house surrounded by a thousand trees
The matriarch in sneakers and a cotton sari
Exercised her rusty bones with reluctance
Under the watchful eyes of her grandchildren

On muted afternoons of pouring rain
'Tell us a story', her grandchildren would say
They would sit close to her and draw comfort
From her distinct scent of Yardley's powder

In the evenings, she sat in her favorite chair
Looking out at trees of mangos and pears
She reserved her evenings for nostalgia
And talked of her childhood in Calcutta

Quiet afternoons, the wave of Dhaka cotton
The ring of a prayer bell, the cooking of mutton
Are moments preserved for memories
Of the matriarch and their favorite stories

Loving you

Loving you takes place
In interludes
In certain lights of day
Notes of music
Anecdotes
Loving you is
A ceaselessly crashing wave

Haiku 1

25

Still afternoon light
Life retreats behind curtains
Silent floors wither

Haiku 2

Darkening June sky
Smelt of new rains and warm plants
Earth groping for roots

One day

27

Maybe one day we will meet
under a casual peach sky
amidst casual passerby's
and we will smile like we didn't
break each other once

www.ingramcontent.com/pod-product-compliance
Lightning Source LLC
LaVergne TN
LVHW021331200726
843509LV00014B/2484